Biblical Uses of Colors and Flags

Sharon S. Busby

Copyright © 2001 Sharon S Busby

All rights reserved.

ISBN-13: 978-1-888081-01-5

This book or parts thereof may not be reproduced in any form without prior written permission of the publisher.

Unless otherwise quoted, all Scripture quotations are taken from the
King James Version of the Bible.

Published by

Good News Fellowship Ministries

220 Sleepy Creek Road

Macon GA 31210

(478)757-8071

http://KathieWaltersMinistry.com

DEDICATION

This book is dedicated to my husband Keith Busby, who has supported me in this book and making and selling flags. He has always loved and encouraged me.

Biblical Uses of Colors and Flags

CONTENTS

	Acknowledgments	i
1	The Biblical Meanings of Colors	Pg 1
2	Combinations of Colors	Pg 21
3	The Biblical References to Banners and Flags	Pg 23
4	Bibliography and Sources	Pg 29

Acknowledgments

Worshipping with flags was a new experience for Sharon Busby. She received a flag as a gift at church about fifteen years ago and has been using them ever since. Sharon made flags for her niece and herself and then gave others away. After a time, people started asking her to make them a flag also.

She has seen discouragement flee from a meeting after the Spirit directed her to walk around the room waving her flag and praying in tongues. Another time she called down the gifts in a meeting and saw each gift exercised in turn, by people acting outside their own comfort zone. She was thrilled another morning, when one of the men from her small group joined all the girls with a beautiful gold flag - he was definitely out of his comfort zone, but loves the Lord.

Flag ministry is to express the heart of a worshiper, not a performer. One must be willing to lay down all gifts and talents so that they can be developed to glorify God. We want to express the mind and heart of worship. Prayer and study of the Word are required in order to bring the anointing which ushers in the very presence of God.

1 BIBLICAL MEANINGS OF COLORS

"Color Awareness in Biblical Literature The writers of biblical literature reflected little or nothing of an abstract sense of color. Nevertheless, they made frequent references to a select group of colors when their purposes in writing so demanded it."

"References to Colors in the Bible Moving beyond color in the abstract sense, one does find in the Bible frequent references to certain objects which have color designations. When reference is made to a particular color or colors, it is likely made for one of two basic reasons. First, a writer may wish to use color in a descriptive sense to help identify an object or clarify some aspect about that object."

"A second reason for color designations in the Bible involves a more specialized usage. At times a writer may use color in a symbolic sense to convey theological truth about the subject of his writing. Color designations have general symbolic significance. For instance, white may be symbolic of purity or joy; black may symbolize judgment or decay; red may symbolize sin or life-blood; and purple may be symbolic of luxury and elegance. Color symbolism became for the writers of apocalyptic literature (Daniel, Revelation) an appropriated tool for expressing various truths in hidden language. In their writings one may find white representative of conquest or victory, black representative of famine or pestilence, red representative of wartime bloodshed, paleness (literally "greenish-gray") representative of death, and purple representative of royalty." "Color Designations of Frequent Use The color designations which appear in the Bible offer relatively little in the way of variety. The matter is further complicated by the fact that of those colors which appears precise translation of the underlying Hebrew and

Greek terms is difficult."

"The colors mentioned most frequently in the Bible are those which refer to the dyed products manufactured by the peoples of Israel and her neighbors. Particularly common are the varying shades in the red-purple range. Purple was the most valued of the ancient dyes and was used in the coloring of woven materials. The peoples of Crete, Phoenicia and Canaan produced the dye from Mollusks taken form the Mediterranean Sea. Purple is noted to be the color of some of the tabernacle furnishings and priests' garments in the Old Testament (Ex. 26:1; 28:4-6). In the New Testament the robe put on Christ and Lydia's occupation are associated with the color purple as well (Mark 15:17; Acts 16:14). By varying the dye-making process, other shades of blue become possible and are noted in Scripture (Ex. 28:5-6; Ezek. 23:6; Rev. 9:17)."

"Shades of Red Dye were produced from the bodies of insects, vegetables, and reddish-colored minerals. These were, likewise used to color garments. In addition, natural objects are sometimes designated red, scarlet, or crimson, including such items as pottage, wine, the sky and horses (Gen. 25:30 Prov. 23:31; Matt. 16:2-3; Rev, 6:4) Isaiah used the color red as a symbol of the nature of sin. (Isa. 1:18)."

"The neutrals, white and black, are mentioned on occasion in the Bible. Natural objects such as milk, leprous skin, and snow are designated white(Gen. 49:12; Lev. 13:3-4; Isa. 1:18). White is used in the New Testament of the garments of Jesus and angels to indicate the glory of the wearer (Matt. 17:2; 28:3; Acts 1:10)/ Natural objects designated black in the Bible include such items as hair, skin, the sky, and even the sun itself (Lev. 13:31; Job 30:30' I Kings 18:45; Rev. 6:12)."

"Other color designations used less frequently but not any less significantly in the Bible are green, yellow, vermilion, and gray. James Sexton"[1]

[1] Trent C. Butler, PH. D, ed. Holman Bible Dictionary. (Nashville TN: Holman Bible Publishers, 1991) pp. 276-277

Smith's Bible Dictionary has this entry:
"Colors
The terms relative to color, occurring in the Bible, may be arranged in two classes, the first including those applied to the description of natural objects, the second those artificial mixtures which were employed in dyeing or painting. The purple and the blue were derived from a small shellfish found in the Mediterranean, and were very costly, and hence they were the royal colors. Red, both scarlet and crimson, was derived from an insect resembling the cochineal. The natural colors noticed in the Bible are white, black, red, yellow and green. The only fundamental color of which the Hebrews appear to have had a clear conception was red ; and even this is not very often noticed."

http://bible.crosswalk.com/Dictionaries/SmithsBibleDictionary/smt.cgi?number=T1049

Nave's Topical Bible has this entry: Colors "Symbolical uses of BLACK: A SYMBOL OF AFFLICTION AND CALAMITY --- Job 3:5; 10:20-22; 30:26; Psalms 107:10, 11; 143:3;

Isaiah 5:30; 8:22; 9:19; 24:11; 50:3; Joel 2:6, 10; 3:14, 15; Amos 5:8; Nahum 2:10; Zeph. 1:14, 15; Matthew 8:12; 22:13; 25:30; 2 Peter 2:4; Jude 1:13; Revelation 16:10."3

Black --- Righteous Judgement, Death, Mourning, Sin and Famine from: Lamentations 4:8 and Revelation 6:5 Repentance; Omnipotence of God; Humiliation; Affliction; Calamity - Lam 4:8; Death - Jer. 8:21; Sin - John 3:19-20; Jer. 14:2 Ps 18:9-11; Terror - Rev 6:5; Endlessness of Space.

"BLUE: SYMBOL OF DEITY --- Exodus 24:10; 25:3, 4; 26:1; 28:28, 37; 38:18; 39:1-5, 21, 24, 29, 31; Numbers 4:5-12; 15:38-40; 2 Chronicles 2:7, 14; 3:14; Jer. 10:9; Ezekiel 1:26; 10:1

SYMBOL OF ROYALTY Esther 8:15; Ezekiel 23:6"3

Blue ---Revelation(color of God); the Spiritual or Heavenly Realm, Exodus 24:10, Ezekiel 1:26, 10:1; Healing; Hope; Grace; Freedom; Holy Spirit & Anointing; Peace; Illumination. Symbol of heaven and authority. Numbers 15:38.

Royal Blue --- God's Commandments Num. 15:38.

Light Blue --- Heaven, Heavenly Ezek. 1:26.

Sapphire Blue(navy) --- Heavenly, the Throne; Divine Revelation Ezek. 1:26, Ex 24:10.

"CRIMSON, RED, PURPLE, AND SCARLET, SYMBOLS OF VARIOUS IDEAS:

Of iniquity --- Isaiah 1:18; Revelation 17:3, 4; 18:12, 16 **Of royalty** --- Judges 8:26; Daniel 5:7, 16, 29; Matthew 27:28 **Prosperity** --- 2 Samuel 1:24; Proverbs 31:21; Lamentations 4:5 **Conquest** --- Nahum 2:3; Revelation 12:3

"These colors figured largely in the symbolism of the tabernacle furnishing, and priestly vestments and functions, as types

and shadows of the atonement - Exodus 25:3-5; 26:1, 14, 31, 36; 36:8, 19, 35, 37; 27:16; 28:4-8, 15, 31, 33; 35:5-7, 23, 25, 35; 38:18, 23; 39:2, 3, 5, 29; Leviticus 14:4, 6,

49, 51, 52; Numbers 4:7, 8, 13; 19:2, 5, 6; Isaiah 63:1-3; Hebrews 9:19-23."[3]

Red --- The Blood of Jesus; Love; Fountain of Forgiveness; Healing; Fire; Deliverance; Passover, Protection
Ex. 12:23.(color of Man). War, Bloodshed, and Death (Also War in the Heavenly)from: 2 Kings 3:21-23, Revelation 6:4, 12:3-8, Nahum 2:3.

(Deep)crimson or Scarlet --- Blood Atonement, Sacrifice of Christ's Blood from Sin and Death Leviticus 14:52, Isaiah 1:18, Hebrews 9:14, Numbers 19:6, Matt. 27:28 Color of the Holy Spirit From: Acts 1:3-4; Consuming Fire. Joshua 2:18-21.

Wine or Deep Red --- Covenant Luke 22:20; Holy Spirit Eph. 5:18.

Burgundy --- The Red Earth; Selfish; Covetous Sin.

Pink --- Right Relationship with God; Power; Healing; Innocence; Faith.

Rose --- The Father's Heavenly Care.

When You Mix Red & Blue You Get

Purple - When You Mix the Blood of Man with God You Get Royalty!!!!

Purple --- Kingship; Royalty - John 19:2; Majesty; Passion; Authority. Jesus Being King of Kings - Jdg. 8:26; Believer's Royalty & Priesthood - 1 Peter 2:9; Rev 19:11-16, John 19:2 & Judges 8:26.

Purple (Dark) --- Royalty, wealth From: Judges 8:26, Song of Songs 3:10, John 19:2

Purple (Pale) --- Penitence and Sorrow From: Mark 15:17, 2 Corinthians 7:10.

Hyacinth --- Holy Spirit; Reward; Divine Revelation.

"**WHITE:** SYMBOL OF HOLINESS The high priest's holy garments were made of white linen --- Leviticus 16:4,32

Choir singers were arrayed in white --- 2 Chronicles 5:12

"**SCRIPTURES EMPLOYING THE SYMBOL** Psalms 51:7; Ecc. 9:8; Isaiah 1:18; Daniel 7:9; 11:35; 12:10; Matthew

17:1, 2; 28:2, 3; Mark 9:3; Revelation 1:13, 14; 2:17; 3:4, 5, 18; 4:4; 6:2, 11; 7:9, 13, 14; 15:6; 19:8, 11, 14; 20:11"[3]

[3]http://bible.crosswalk.com/Concordances/NavesTopicalBible/ntb.cgi?number=T1184

White --- (Contains all colors) --- Purity, righteousness acquired through the blood, Christ, angels, saints, color of the creator from: Revelation 6;2, 19:8, 7:9, 4:4, 3:18, Ecc. 9:8, Matthew 17:2, 28:3, Acts 1:10, Daniel 7:9, Isaiah 1:18

The Bride - Rev 3:5, 7:9.19:8; Purity - Dan 12:10; the Heavenly, Angelic Realm; Light - Dan 7:9; Holiness- Matt. 17:2; Resurrection - Zech. 6:3; Overcomer, Triumph - John 20:12; Ps 27:1, Dan 7:9. White Robe of Righteousness(Priestly Garments), Rev 1:4.

Green: --- New Life, Growth, Prosperity, Flourish, Ps 92:14, Fruitfulness; Praise; Resting in God; Color of the Trinity From: Psalm 23:2, Genesis 1:30, Luke 23:31, Mark 6:39 Tribe of Judah - Life; Health. Ps 92:14 Ps 1:3 Life Everlasting 1 John 5:12.

Posterity Ps 37:35.

Emerald --- Presence; the Throne Room of God; Mercy From: Revelation 4:3.

Green (Pale): pale horse --- yellowish-green death and disease from: Revelation 6:8.

Greenish Turquoise --- Tribe of Naphtali; Dividing Flesh and Spirit.

Brown --- Man as we are; Earth - Gen. 1:10; dark earth colors, wood Humanity --- 1 Cor. 15:47 Ex 26:15 Godly Offspring --- Is 11:1. Jer. 23:5. Uncleanness; Associated with Sorrow or Disease.

Cream --- Healing.

Tan --- Bread, Communion, Y'shua(Jesus' Body) Luke 22:19.

Orange --- Warfare Intercession; Praise; Spiritual Courage; Boldness; Intimacy; Companionship with God; the Tribe of Gad -Ps 150, Eph. 6:10-20.

Yellow --- Joy; Sunlight of Jesus, joyous from: Matthew 17:2, Revelation 1:16 and

Psalm 84:11; God's Glory Ezek. 1:4-8:2, Ps 68:13. Associated With "Green", Can Mean "Putting Forth" and Sprouting. May Also Refer to (Yellow continued) Sickness, Disease and Rottenness.

Amber --- Glory of God - Ezek. 1:4, 8:2.

Silver --- price paid for redemption - atoning for the soul from: Matthew 27:3, 1 Peter 1:18, Numbers 3:44-51 Zech. 11:12, 13, Exodus 30:11-16, Strength; Spirit; Revelation & Grace; Purity; Majesty; Redemption - Matt. 27:3-9; God's Word Ps 12:6 Ps 66;10; Symbols of Nobility, Vessels of Sacred Use. Gen. 23:15, Matt. 27:1-9.

Gold --- Power; God's Glory & Divine Nature - Ezra 1:4, 8:2 & Rev 3:18; Might of His people; Holiness, Royalty; from: Rev 4:4, 14:14, Mal. 3:3, Hag. 2:8, Song of Songs 5:1; the Heavenly Realm; Presence of God; Refining; Brilliance; Purity; Righteousness; Represents Choice of Fine Treasure - Acts 17:29; Rev 21:18-23.

Brass --- May Be Rendered Bronze and Sometimes Copper

Brass/copper: judgement against disobedience, heaven, as brass or iron - Christ as Judge of all sin from: Numbers 21:9, Deuteronomy 28:13-23 Revelation 1:12-15; Atonement, Forgiveness - Num. 21:9 May Denote Rot, Rainless Sky; Parches Soil; Baseness as Compared to Rich and Precious Metals. Expresses Physical Strength, Power and Durability. --- Job 6:12, 40:18, 41:27 Ps 107:16

Copper --- Signifies Impurity Due to Alloys - Combines with Zinc & Tin, --- May Represent Strength.

Brazen --- Christ the Cleanser --- I John 4:7.

Bronze --- Judgement on Sin; Fires of Testing Num. 21:7; Tabernacle Altar - Ex 38:30.

Clay --- Type of Fragility Ps 2:9 - Earthen Vessel

Coral --- Something of High Value. Job

28:18; Red Sea, Exodus 15:1 & 21, Deliverance Heb. 11:23.

Crystal --- Overcoming Bride of Christ; Sanctification; Salt of the Earth; Water Baptism --- Matt. 3:11; Durability; Transparency; Wind, Holy spirit, "Born Again" - John 3: 3 & 5-7.

Pearl --- Symbol of God's truth - purity, God's people formed through suffering: Matthew 11:45, 46 Treasure, Reward, Gate, Doorway - Matt. 13:44-46, Rev 21:21; Symbol of Suffering.

Iridescent --- Cleansing Work of the Holy Spirit; Blessings of God; Angel Wings; Overcoming Power, Fruit of the Spirit from: Revelation 4:3 Overcomer - Rev 21:7, 27.

Fire --- the Consuming Fire of God; Sacrifice of Prayer Heb. 13:15; Praise & Worship. Chron. 23:13; Revival Fire; Refiner's Fire- 1 Cor. 3:13; the Passion of Jesus for His Bride; the Bride's Response of Passion for Jesus.

Shekinah --- Holy Spirit.

Rainbow --- God's Promises - Rev 4:3; Covenant - Gen. 9:13, 16.

All Colors --- Jubilee - Lev. 25:9-10

Star of David --- Represents Israel and praying for the peace of Jerusalem, Israel - Ps 122:6

Biblical Uses of Colors and Flags

2 COMBINATION OF COLORS

Colors Can Be Used in Combination to Symbolize Various Biblical Truths

The Royally of Christ The priesthood of Believers - Plum, Grape Purple Orchid, & White - Rev 1:6

Holy Fire/Baptism of the Holy Spirit - Wine, Orange, Red, Yellow, & White - Acts 2:3.4

Covenant --- Red, Yellow, Blue, Orange, Green, Purple - Genesis 9:13

Tabernacle --- Gold, Bronze, Purple, White, Scarlet Blue, & Silver --- Ex 25:I-8 23:5-12

Bride --- White, Silver, Iridescence, & slight Pink for the healing of the wounds of the bride.

Warfare --- Black, Gold and Red.

Royalty --- *Purple & Red*

River of God --- Blue, Aqua & Sliver

Majesty --- Purple, Red & Gold

Fire of God --- Gold, Red & Yellow

Israel --- Silver & Blue

Rainbow --- Glory of the Lord Covenant Promise Red, Yellow, Orange, Purple, Blue, & Green - Ezek. 1:28; Gen. 9:13

Intercession --- White Silver, & Gold

This Is a combination of several different teachings on colors. There an some minor variations as you can see, but remember as an extension of His overwhelmingly creative nature, God often uses color to express Himself, We too can express ourselves in different colors, In who we are and what we believe!

3 BIBLICAL REFERENCES TO BANNERS & FLAGS

A Banner is used as a signal, standard, Identification mark like an emblem or color. It rallies the troops and it can mean to flaunt or to be conspicuous. "We will lift up banners in the name of our God" - Psalm 20:5 SOS 6:4 Num. 2:2

Ps 20:5 (KJV) "We will rejoice in thy salvation, and in the name of our God we will set up our banners: the Lord fulfil all thy petitions."

SS 6:4 (NLT) "O my beloved, you are as beautiful as the lovely town of Tirzah. Yes, as beautiful as Jerusalem! You are as majestic as an army with banners!"

Num 2:2 (NIV) "The Israelites are to camp around the Tent of Meeting some distance from it, each man under his standard with the banners of his family."

Isa. 13:2 (NLT) "See the flags waving as the enemy attacks. Cheer them on, O Israel! Wave to them as they march against Babylon to destroy the palaces of the high and mighty."

Isa. 18:3 "When I raise my battle flag on the mountain, let all the world take notice. When I blow the trumpet, listen!

Isa. 31:9 Even their generals will quake with terror and flee when they see the battle flags, says the Lord, whose flame burns brightly in Jerusalem."

Isa. 62:10 "Go out! Prepare the highway for my people to return! Smooth out the road; pull out the boulders; raise a flag for all the nations to see."

Jer. 51:12 "Raise the battle flag against Babylon! Reinforce the guard and station the. watchmen. Prepare an ambush, for the Lord will fulfill all his plans against Babylon."

Standard is a figure adopted an as emblem by a people, like the eagle for the United States. Standard Is also an example or model: Ex 17:9-12 John 15:13

We display banners because of truth Banners must always represent TRUTH because Jesus Is TRUTH Ps. 60:41

Nes from nasas (Strongs 5251) - to be high or conspicuous Is 26:11 Your hand is lifted (as in raise banner) up yet they do not see it.

Jehovah Nissi translated means "God Is my banner" - Ex 17:15

Degel (Strongs 1713/1714) - to carry or set up banner Nu. 2:2 Song Sol 2:4 awesome as an army with banners. Serpent set on a standard Nu. 21: 8, 9 Isa. 31:9 Princes terrified at the standard

He will raise a flag among the nations for Israel to rally around. He will gather the scattered people of Judah from the ends of the earth. Is 11:10, 12

Owth (Strongs 226) means signal. Banners to gather/assemble Joel 2:1-11

What God has called me to - Demons know their ranks - so must the Child of God. We must not give up our position - they don't give up. Got to Know where you stand! We are pointing people to Jesus in our Praise & worship.

John 12:32 Jesus said, "And I, if I be lifted up; shall draw all men unto Myself."

And as we lift up His name we are using the banners.

Judgest as the children of Israel did:

1. As a visual demonstration of God's presence --- Is 62:10-12 (Quoted on page)

2. As a sign of victory --- Ex 17:15

3. A sign of Identification --- Nu. 2:2 (show whose we are)

4. Praise --- Ps. 20:5 (Quoted on page 23)

After the battle with Amalek - Moses built an altar and called It "Jehovah Nissi" - The Lord My Banner. Whenever God reveals one of His names through scripture, He reveals something of significance concerning His character and His Power in the heavenlies. The lifting of banners is very much a God-ordained practice - it is figuratively a demonstration of the presence of God being lifted in our midst.

The cross became the pole - Jesus was lifted, a Jehovah Nissi, the banner, and the heavens were shaken by the glory of God which was lifted high in all the earth. Whenever we lift a banner, and lift Christ in our hearts, then there is much more happening than a piece of wood and cloth being raised - something happens in the heavenlies - whenever Christ is lifted.

Something happens when a banner is lifted - there is a call and a cry to gather, there is a drawing and a point of focus. When we raise our banner, great indignation and reproach is kindled in the hearts of the enemy. Satan cannot stand it when we lift the banners - the glory of God is displayed in the midst of His people. We can march with banners and claim great victory! Look beyond the sign and behold your God.

The banner is used to draw our hearts towards God and to see things and enter into things that are deeper than those on an earthly plane.

"From children and infants You have ordained praise" - Ps 8:2

THE MAJORITY OF THIS SECTION ON BANNERS AND FLAGS WAS DONE BY MRS. PEGGY JONES OF PERRY, GA - A FRIEND WHO GAVE ME MY FIRST TWO FLAGS. ONLY THE LORD KNEW HOW BADLY I WANTED ONE AND PEGGY LISTENED TO HIS PROMPTING.

[4] BIBLIOGRAPHY & SOURCES

[1]Trent C. Butler, PH. D, ed. Holman Bible Dictionary. (Nashville TN: Holman Bible Publishers, 1991)
pp. 276-277

[2]Smith's Bible Dictionary: Colors
http://bible.crosswalk.com/Dictionaries/SmithsBibleDictionary/smt.cgi?number=T1049

[3]Nave's Topical Bible: Colors
http://bible.crosswalk.com/Concordances/NavesTopicalBible/ntb.cgi?number=T1184

Color & Color Combination information sheets,
Joyful Life Ministries, JoAnne Ferderer,
St Paul MN

Color & Flag information sheets.
Mrs. Peggy Jones, Perry GA

Biblical references flags, colors
http.www.Jehovahnissi.freeserve.co.uk

Colors list, Flag ministry,
NorthGate Church of Atlanta

Made in the USA
Columbia, SC
10 June 2019